In Celebration Of

_____

_____

Date

_____

Location

_____

Guests

Thoughts & Best Wishes

Guests

Thoughts & Best Wishes

_____

_____

_____

_____

_____

_____

_____

_____

_____

_____

_____

Guests

Thoughts & Best Wishes

Guests

Thoughts & Best Wishes

_____

_____

_____

_____

_____

_____

_____

_____

_____

_____

_____

_____

_____

Guests

Thoughts & Best Wishes

_____

_____

_____

_____

_____

_____

_____

_____

_____

_____

_____

_____

Guests

Thoughts & Best Wishes

Guests

Thoughts & Best Wishes

Guests

Thoughts & Best Wishes

Guests

Thoughts & Best Wishes

Guests

Thoughts & Best Wishes

Guests

Thoughts & Best Wishes

Guests

Thoughts & Best Wishes

Guests

Thoughts & Best Wishes

Guests

Thoughts & Best Wishes

Guests

Thoughts & Best Wishes

Guests

Thoughts & Best Wishes

Guests

Thoughts & Best Wishes

Guests

Thoughts & Best Wishes

Guests

Thoughts & Best Wishes

Guests

Thoughts & Best Wishes

Guests

Thoughts & Best Wishes

Guests

Thoughts & Best Wishes

Guests

Thoughts & Best Wishes

Guests

Thoughts & Best Wishes

_____

_____

_____

_____

_____

_____

_____

_____

_____

_____

_____

_____

_____

Guests

Thoughts & Best Wishes

Guests

Thoughts & Best Wishes

Guests

Thoughts & Best Wishes

_____

_____

_____

_____

_____

_____

_____

_____

_____

_____

_____

_____

Guests

Thoughts & Best Wishes

Guests

Thoughts & Best Wishes

Guests

Thoughts & Best Wishes

Guests

Thoughts & Best Wishes

Guests

Thoughts & Best Wishes

_____

_____

_____

_____

_____

_____

_____

_____

_____

_____

_____

_____

_____

Guests

Thoughts & Best Wishes

Guests

Thoughts & Best Wishes

Guests

Thoughts & Best Wishes

Guests

Thoughts & Best Wishes

Guests

Thoughts & Best Wishes

Guests

Thoughts & Best Wishes

Guests

Thoughts & Best Wishes

Guests

Thoughts & Best Wishes

Guests

Thoughts & Best Wishes

_____

_____

_____

_____

_____

Guests

Thoughts & Best Wishes

Guests

Thoughts & Best Wishes

Guests

Thoughts & Best Wishes

Guests

Thoughts & Best Wishes

_____

_____

_____

_____

_____

_____

_____

_____

_____

_____

_____

_____

_____

Guests

Thoughts & Best Wishes

Guests

Thoughts & Best Wishes

Guests

Thoughts & Best Wishes

Guests

Thoughts & Best Wishes

Made in the USA
Middletown, DE
11 May 2022